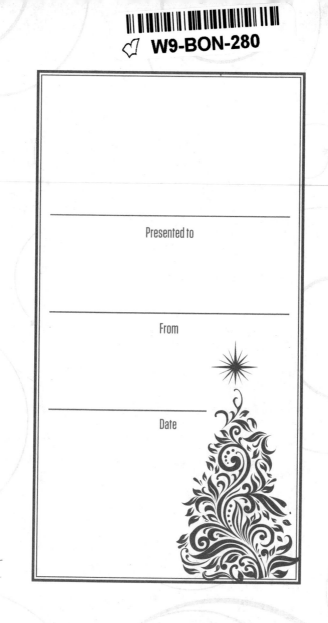

W9-BON-280

Presented to

From

Date

December 2017

THE PROMISE *of* CHRISTMAS IS JESUS

JACK COUNTRYMAN

COUNTRYMAN ®

A Division of Thomas Nelson Publishers

THOMAS NELSON
Since 1798

NASHVILLE   DALLAS   MEXICO CITY   RIO DE JANEIRO

The Promise of Christmas Is Jesus
© 2012 Jack Countryman

Published in Nashville, Tennessee, by Thomas Nelson. Thomas Nelson is a registered trademark of Thomas Nelson, Inc.

Thomas Nelson, Inc., titles may be purchased in bulk for educational, business, fund-raising, or sales promotional use. For information, please e-mail SpecialMarkets@ThomasNelson.com.

Scripture quotations are taken from THE NEW KING JAMES VERSION. © 1982 by Thomas Nelson, Inc. Used by permission. All rights reserved.

ISBN-13: 978-1-4003-2118-6
ISBN-13: 978-1-4003-2085-1 (with display)

Printed in the United States of America

12 13 14 15 16 DP 5 4 3 2 1

www.thomasnelson.com

God makes a promise.

Faith believes His promise.

Hope anticipates its fulfillment.

Patience quietly waits.

Contents

Introduction

God's Gifts and Promises for Christmas

❦

Christmas is a season of celebrating the birth of our Savior and a time of sharing gifts with those we cherish and love. *The Promise of Christmas* has been created to draw attention to the wonderful gift of God's promises for everyone who walks with God. As you read and ponder these promises of God, pray that each passage will equip you to live in such a way that God will be glorified and you will have the joy and peace that passes all understanding.

The Christmas Story

It's a timeless story—the account of Jesus' birth—with familiar details such as shepherds, a star, wise men, and angels. But perhaps the details, if not the story itself, are too familiar. Are we any longer able to hear the wonder of this world-changing, history-altering story?

God planned the birth of Jesus before time began, and throughout the Old Testament—thousands of years before a Baby was born in Bethlehem—God hinted about the coming of this Messiah, this King of kings, Lord of lords, Prince of Peace.

Looking at these hints—these ancient prophecies—and their fulfillment in the New Testament accounts of Jesus' birth can help us recapture the wonder of the Christmas story and marvel at the gift of Jesus, a gift of sacrifice and love, of Immanuel, "God with us."

May seeing the promises of God and their fulfillment reignite in you the very *hope of Christmas.*

It came to pass in those days that a decree went out from Caesar Augustus that all the world should be registered. This census first took place while Quirinius was governing Syria. So all went to be registered, everyone to his own city.

Joseph also went up from Galilee, out of the city of Nazareth, into Judea, to the city of David, which is called Bethlehem, because he was of the house and lineage of David, to be registered with Mary, his betrothed wife, who was with child. So it was, that while they were there, the days were completed for her to be delivered. And she brought forth her firstborn Son, and wrapped Him in swaddling cloths, and laid Him in a manger, because there was no room for them in the inn.

Now there were in the same country shepherds living out in the fields, keeping watch over their flock by night. And behold, an angel of the Lord stood before them, and the glory of the Lord shone around them, and they were greatly afraid. Then the angel said to them, "Do not be afraid, for behold, I bring you good tidings of great joy which will be to all people. For there is born to you this day in the city of David a Savior, who is Christ the Lord. And this will be the sign to you: You will find a Babe wrapped in swaddling cloths, lying in a manger."

And suddenly there was with the angel a multitude of the heavenly host praising God and saying:

> "Glory to God in the highest,
> And on earth peace, goodwill
> toward men!"

Luke 2:1–14

AWAY
in a
MANGER

ANONYMOUS

Away in a manger, no crib for a bed,
The little Lord Jesus laid down His sweet
head.
The stars in the sky looked down where
He lay,
The little Lord Jesus, asleep on the hay.

The cattle are lowing, the Baby awakes
But little Lord Jesus, no crying He makes.
I love Thee, Lord Jesus; look down from
the sky,
And stay by my cradle till morning is
nigh.

Be near me, Lord Jesus; I ask Thee to stay
Close by me forever and love me, I pray.
Bless all the dear children in Thy tender
care,
And take us to heaven to live with Thee
there.

God's Promise to Mary

—~ ✳ ~—

"Blessed is she who believed, for there will be a
fulfillment of those things which were told her
from the Lord."

And Mary said:
> *"My soul magnifies the Lord,*
> *And my spirit has rejoiced in God my Savior.*
> *For He has regarded the lowly state of His*
> *   maidservant;*
> *For behold, henceforth all generations*
> *   will call me blessed.*
> *For He who is mighty has done great*
> *   things for me,*
> *And holy is His name.*
> *And His mercy is on those who fear Him*
> *From generation to generation.*
> *He has shown strength with His arm;*
> *He has scattered the proud in the imagina-*
> *   tion of their hearts.*
> *He has put down the mighty from their thrones,*
> *And exalted the lowly.*
> *He has filled the hungry with good things,*

And the rich He has sent away empty.
He has helped His servant Israel,
In remembrance of His mercy,
As He spoke to our fathers,
To Abraham and to his seed forever."

Luke 1:45–55

*F*rom all appearances, Mary was an ordinary girl living in a one-stoplight town—when an amazing moment revealed both her extraordinary character and her uncommon faith in her unseen and ever-faithful God. Believing the angel's outrageous claim that she would give birth to God's Son and completely trusting that the Almighty would enable her to walk that path, Mary yielded her life—her very body—to her Creator. Despite the cost to her, despite the public shame and her derailed dreams, Mary was a model of humble and willing submission to the Lord's plans, and the world has celebrated her obedience to God for more than two thousand years.

The Word Became Flesh

~~~ ✳ ~~~

*H*ave you ever received a one-of-a-kind gift? Something unique, completely unlike anything you had ever seen or even heard of? When the apostle John referred to Jesus as the "only begotten of the Father," the original Greek means "unique" or "one-of-a-kind." And as God's gift to us, Jesus—who is both fully God and fully man—is indeed unique.

Yet, as the Lamb of God who died on the cross on behalf of sinful humanity, Jesus is not a gift to be hoarded. What will you do to share your one-of-a-kind gift of Jesus with someone this season?

In the beginning was the Word, and the Word was with God, and the Word was God. He was in the beginning with God. All things were made through Him, and without Him nothing was made that was made. In Him was life, and the life was the light of men. And the light shines in the darkness, and the darkness did not comprehend it. . . . And the Word became flesh and dwelt among us, and we beheld His glory, the glory as of the only begotten of the Father, full of grace and truth.

John 1:1–5, 14

The Gift of Jesus the Messiah

❦

*T*he Son of God, eternal throughout time, infinite in every way, entered the confines of a twenty-four-hour day and the finiteness of a human body in order to dwell among us. And He would do more—far more—than visit and observe. Jesus left His Father's side, took on human flesh, and walked among us in order to die for us.

And God had spoken through prophets to call people to watch for the coming Messiah. He sent angels to announce Jesus' birth, and Jesus revealed His identity through His signs and miracles and teaching—and His death and resurrection. Yet many people missed Him—and still miss Him today.

The night our Savior was born in Bethlehem was a night like many others before it—but unlike any night since. Would you have recognized its significance? And whom will you help recognize it even now, two thousand years later?

He is the image of the invisible God, the firstborn over all creation. For by Him all things were created that are in heaven and that are on earth, visible and invisible, whether thrones or dominions or principalities or powers. All things were created through Him and for Him. And He is before all things, and in Him all things consist. And He is the head of the body, the church, who is the beginning, the firstborn from the dead, that in all things He may have the preeminence.

Colossians 1:15–18

Immanuel, "God with Us"

———— ✳ ————

 *S*he was favored; we are blessed. Mary yielded her life, her dreams, her very body to the Sovereign and His plan for all humanity. The Holy God, who had been immeasurably far away since our first mother and father sinned in the garden, would come to earth through young Mary's holy womb and be Immanuel, "God with us."

Some people will make their annual or semiannual visit to church in honor of this God who has come near. But if this Babe truly is God, does He not deserve more attention than Christmas Eve and perhaps Easter Sunday? Jesus has come close for a reason. Actually, for several reasons. He wants His wandering sheep—sinful human beings—to recognize their sin, receive His forgiveness, and live with Him, now and for eternity, as Lord of their lives. Jesus has come near to bless us with His grace, to guide us, to protect us, to provide for us, to free us from our sinful ways and their consequences, and to show us and tell us that He loves us.

Receive Jesus' love if you haven't. Share His love if you have.

So all this was done that it might be fulfilled which was spoken by the Lord through the prophet, saying: "Behold, the virgin shall be with child, and bear a Son, and they shall call His name Immanuel," which is translated, "God with us."

**Matthew
1:22–23**

O COME, O Come, EMMANUEL

NINTH-CENTURY LATIN HYMN
TRANSLATED BY JOHN M. NEALE

O come, O come, Emmanuel,
And ransom captive Israel,
That mourns in lonely exile here
Until the Son of God appear.

Rejoice! Rejoice! Emmanuel
Shall come to thee, O Israel!

O come, Thou Wisdom from on high,
Who orderest all things mightily;
To us the path of knowledge show
And teach us in her ways to go.

Rejoice! Rejoice! Emmanuel
Shall come to thee, O Israel!

O come, Desire of Nations, bind
In one the hearts of all mankind.
Bid Thou our sad divisions cease,
And be Thyself our King of Peace.

Rejoice! Rejoice! Emmanuel
Shall come to thee, O Israel!

O come, Thou Dayspring, come and cheer
Our spirits by Thine advent here;
Disperse the gloomy clouds of night,
And death's dark shadows put to flight.

Rejoice! Rejoice! Emmanuel
Shall come to thee, O Israel!

Unchanging God

———— ✳ ————

What Christmas traditions do you enjoy? Maybe you always bake cookies, decorate the tree at a specific time, or read the Christmas story before you open gifts—and maybe you've been doing these things for years, if not generations. But maybe some traditions have changed with time. The rich, buttery cookies Great-Grandma baked have been replaced by healthier oatmeal bars, or the tree gets decorated whenever a large group of family members is under the roof at the same time.

Unlike some of our Christmas traditions, our God does not change from year to year, from generation to generation, or even from century to century. He who came as a Baby to the manger in Bethlehem still comes to us—as risen King—whatever our humble circumstances. May we, in turn, go out to others in His name to share His love and grace.

Praise the LORD, all you Gentiles!
Laud Him, all you peoples!
For His merciful kindness is great toward us,
And the truth of the LORD endures forever.

Praise the LORD!

Psalm 117:1–2

Blessed be the name of the LORD
From this time forth and forevermore!
From the rising of the sun to its going down
The LORD's name is to be praised.

The LORD is high above all nations,
His glory above the heavens.

Psalm 113:2–4

God's Favor

———— ✳ ————

*W*hether we do someone a favor or show someone favor, we are freely giving of our love, our time, our finances, our possessions. But giving freely does not mean the gift itself was free. When God shows us His favor—when He offers His forgiveness, His love, His mercy, His grace, His protection, His provision—He does so freely, but that favor did not come cheap. It cost Jesus His life.

Having invested His own Son's life on our behalf, God continually pours out His favor on those who recognize the sacrifice of the cross. In the words of the psalmist, God's favor "will surround [us] as with a shield." Our loving God will bestow His favor upon us through all of life's circumstances. As we receive God's favor—during this blessed season and year-round—may we find ways to share it with those around us.

But let all those rejoice who put their trust in
    You;
Let them ever shout for joy, because You
    defend them;
Let those also who love Your name
Be joyful in You.
*For You, O L*ORD*, will bless the righteous;*
With favor You will surround him as with a
    shield.

Psalm 5:11–12

Blessed is the man who listens to me,
Watching daily at my gates,
Waiting at the posts of my doors.
For whoever finds me finds life,
*And obtains favor from the L*ORD*.*

Proverbs 8:34–35

Spiritual Gifts and Talents

—✳︎—

*J*ohn the Baptist obeyed God's calling to be the messenger who led people to repent and be baptized. Obedient to this calling, John was faithful to the point of losing his life rather than backing down. To God be the glory!

God is still glorified when, like John the Baptist, His people use their spiritual gifts "for the profit of all." God works in each individual to benefit the entire body. And although different tasks within the body call for different gifts, all tasks and gifts have the same goal. At the time when each of us comes to faith in Christ, we receive at least one gift—not merely to build up our own life of faith but also to strengthen unity in the church. Ask God today to show you the gifts and talents given to you by His Spirit. Then use those gifts in the body of Christ as He directs. As you do so, you'll find your faith stretched and strengthened.

There are diversities of gifts, but the same Spirit. There are differences of ministries, but the same Lord. And there are diversities of activities, but it is the same God who works all in all. But the manifestation of the Spirit is given to each one for the profit of all: for to one is given the word of wisdom through the Spirit, to another the word of knowledge through the same Spirit, to another faith by the same Spirit, to another gifts of healings by the same Spirit, to another the working of miracles, to another prophecy, to another discerning of spirits, to another different kinds of tongues, to another the interpretation of tongues. But one and the same Spirit works all these things, distributing to each one individually as He wills.

1 Corinthians 12:4–11

His Blessing

———※———

*O*ur God loves to pour out blessings! He demonstrates His love to those of us who love Him—who show our love by obeying Him—when He provides and protects, when He guides our steps and goes ahead of us, when He walks with us through hard times and brings us to good and pleasant places. God blesses us with His constant presence. Whatever trials we face, nothing can separate us from His love. Whatever twists in the road, nothing can interfere with His sovereign power and goodness. Whatever missteps we take, He can redeem. Whatever hurts we experience, He can heal. Yes, our God loves to pour out blessings!

When God made a promise to Abraham, because He could swear by no one greater, He swore by Himself, saying, "Surely blessing I will bless you, and multiplying I will multiply you." And so, after he had patiently endured, he obtained the promise.

Hebrews 6:13–15

Blessed is the man
Who walks not in the counsel of the ungodly,
    Nor stands in the path of sinners,
    Nor sits in the seat of the scornful;
But his delight is in the law of the LORD,
    And in His law he meditates day
        and night.
He shall be like a tree
    Planted by the rivers of water,
    That brings forth its fruit in its
        season,
    Whose leaf also shall not wither;
And whatever he does shall prosper.

Psalm 1:1–3

His Faithfulness

—✳—

Let us hold fast the confession of our hope without wavering, for He who promised is faithful.

*I*n Hebrews 10:22, God invites us to "draw near" to Him with "a true heart in full assurance of faith." His invitation is grounded in the promise that He—our unchanging Lord—will always be faithful and that His love for us will absolutely never waver. We can therefore hold fast to the hope in our all-loving, all-powerful risen Lord, whose birth we celebrate this season. And may the hope that we have in Jesus Christ flavor our words and our actions so that others may see His grace and love and ask us about His faithfulness. May we have the opportunity this Christmas to share the story of Jesus' birth and the reasons for our hope in Him.

Forever, O Lord,
Your word is settled in heaven.
Your faithfulness endures to all generations;
You established the earth, and it abides.
They continue this day according
    to Your ordinances,
For all are Your servants.

Psalm 119:89–91

Through the Lord's *mercies we are not*
    consumed,
Because His compassions fail not.
They are new every morning;
Great is Your faithfulness.

Lamentations 3:22–23

His Grace

—— ✳ ——

$\mathscr{A}$re you on a quest for that perfect gift for someone you love? If so, you are undoubtedly considering personality, likes, dislikes—and your budget. You may be spending hours, if not days, going from website to website, store to store, sale to sale, trying to find exactly what you're looking for. Why? Because you love that person. Because of the joy you'll experience when you give the gift!

God already has the perfect gift for you, and it is . . . grace. It is a perfect fit. No exchanges are necessary. And it is unique: it comes only from Him through Jesus. In His grace, God accepts you not for who you are or what you have or haven't done, but because of who He is and what He allowed Jesus to do on the cross on your behalf. Yes, it's the perfect gift.

By grace you have been saved through faith, and that not of yourselves; it is the gift of God, not of works, lest anyone should boast. For we are His workmanship, created in Christ Jesus for good works, which God prepared beforehand that we should walk in them.

Ephesians 2:8–10

The Lord God is a sun and shield;
The Lord will give grace and glory;
No good thing will He withhold
From those who walk uprightly.

O Lord of hosts,
Blessed is the man who trusts in
        You!

Psalm 84:11–12

God's Guidance

~~~ ✳ ~~~

Although Jesus remained silent during His kangaroo-court trials, God Himself is not silent. He speaks through Scripture, He comforts by His Spirit, and He will guide continually and satisfy our souls when we choose to walk with Him through life. What a wonderful promise!

The Lord also promises that when we trust in Him with all our heart and allow Him to direct our lives, He will always go before us. The Holy Spirit is our source of truth, and He is with us and within us to guide our steps. Our task is to listen for Him and follow His directions. Continued guidance, a satisfied soul, His strength—what wonderful promises for life!

The Lord will guide you continually,
And satisfy your soul in drought,
And strengthen your bones;
You shall be like a watered garden,
And like a spring of water, whose waters do
  not fail.

Isaiah 58:11

I will instruct you and teach you in the way
  you should go;
I will guide you with My eye.

Psalm 32:8

"When He, the Spirit of truth, has
come, He will guide you into all
truth; for He will not speak on His
own authority, but whatever He
hears He will speak; and He will
tell you things to come."

John 16:13

Day 12

His Mercy

~~~ ✳ ~~~

or every action there is an equal but opposite reaction. This is Sir Isaac Newton's Third Law of Motion and a basic principle of physics. Does it apply in the spiritual realm?

God freely gives us His mercy: an *action*. And what is our *reaction* to His action? Praise—and may it be equal to the weight of His mercy in our lives!

It is God's very nature to give His children mercy and grace—but not because we deserve it. "His mercy endures forever"—and forever is a long time. There is no expiration date. Why does God do this for us? Simply because He loves us.

God sends a sunrise every morning, He listens when we talk, and He gave us His only Son at Christmas. How can we react to God's infinitely gracious actions? With our praises. By worshipping Him with all our heart, soul, mind, and strength. No, that reaction can never equal God's generosity; thankfully, He is more concerned about our hearts than about the laws of physics.

Oh, give thanks to the LORD, for He is good!
For His mercy endures forever.
Let the redeemed of the LORD say so,
Whom He has redeemed from the hand of the enemy,
And gathered out of the lands,
From the east and from the west,
From the north and from the south.

Psalm 107:1–3

Praise the LORD!

Oh, give thanks to the LORD, for He is good!
For His mercy endures forever.

Who can utter the mighty acts of the LORD?
Who can declare all His praise?
Blessed are those who keep justice,
And he who does righteousness at all times!

Psalm 106:1–3

His Forgiveness

—— ✳ ——

*P*aul was a man transformed by God's forgiveness. This good Jew spent the first part of his life persecuting fellow Jews who believed in Jesus—but that was before the risen Lord met him and changed him on the Damascus Road. That began his tutorial in how to live for God.

As Paul later taught, God wants every part of us—body, soul, and spirit—to enter into relationship with Him and to focus on growing close to Him. And because God wants no barriers between us, He will forgive all our sins, and He promises to remember them no more. The forgiveness God has promised to us is irrevocable; when we are genuinely repentant, we receive it.

One more thing: you just may need to seek forgiveness from someone in your circle of family, friends, neighbors, and acquaintances. Remember, it will be a Christmas gift to both of you.

Lord, hear my voice!
Let Your ears be attentive
To the voice of my supplications.

If You, LORD, should mark iniquities,
O Lord, who could stand?
But there is forgiveness with You,
That You may be feared.

I wait for the LORD, my soul waits,
And in His word I do hope.

Psalm 130:2–5

You, being dead in your trespasses
and the uncircumcision of your
flesh, [Jesus] has made alive
together with Him, having forgiven
you all trespasses, having wiped out
the handwriting of requirements
that was against us, which was
contrary to us. And He has taken
it out of the way, having nailed
it to the cross.

Colossians 2:13–14

God's Comfort

———— ✻ ————

*H*ave you noticed that the best source of comfort is someone who has struggled with pain, sorrow, or loss? That is one reason why God offers His followers the gift of comfort, so that we can, in turn, give it to others. Yes, God sometimes allows tragedy to enter our lives, but He never intends for us to go through difficult times alone. Once we have—by God's grace—gone through a dark time, God calls us to offer comfort to the hurting people He puts in our path. Often that comfort is our mere presence, not "right" words. Our willingness to share the kind of comfort we have received reflects both our knowledge of our good God and our faith in Him.

And whether we are receiving or offering comfort, we can rely on the greatest Comforter of all, the Holy Spirit. Given to us by God, the Spirit is continually with us, willing to guide and empower us as we come alongside hurting people. Yes, our

Redeemer-God is at work when He uses the comforted to comfort others!

Blessed be the God and Father of our Lord Jesus Christ, the Father of mercies and God of all comfort, who comforts us in all our tribulation, that we may be able to comfort those who are in any trouble, with the comfort with which we ourselves are comforted by God. For as the sufferings of Christ abound in us, so our consolation also abounds through Christ. Now if we are afflicted, it is for your consolation and salvation, which is effective for enduring the same sufferings which we also suffer. Or if we are comforted, it is for your consolation and salvation. And our hope for you is steadfast, because we know that as you are partakers of the sufferings, so also you will partake of the consolation.

2 Corinthians 1:3–7

God's Goodness

———※———

*S*urely goodness and mercy shall follow me all the days of my life"? Certain days—certain seasons of life—may cause us to question God's goodness, His mercy, and even His presence with us. In times like that, we choose to believe this truth David proclaimed. We choose to trust that God is with us and is choreographing good to come as a result of these dark places. We choose to believe—regardless of our circumstances—that Jesus, our Good Shepherd, is with us and is caring for us. After all, God promises us not just joy in His blessed presence for eternity but joy in this life as well. So choose to be aware of and to savor His goodness to you in this life. Thank Him continually for being your Good Shepherd, for knowing you by name, and for guiding your steps.

The LORD is my shepherd;
I shall not want.
He makes me to lie down in green pastures;
He leads me beside the still waters.
He restores my soul;
He leads me in the paths of righteousness
For His name's sake.

Yea, though I walk through the valley of the
    shadow of death,
I will fear no evil;
For You are with me;
Your rod and Your staff, they comfort me.

You prepare a table before me in
    the presence of my enemies;
You anoint my head with oil;
My cup runs over.
Surely goodness and mercy shall
    follow me
All the days of my life;
And I will dwell in the house of
    the LORD
Forever.

Psalm 23

His Compassion

— ✳ —

ortgages, car loans, credit cards—
we may feel as though we can never
cover all our debts! One of our debts, however, has been paid in full by One who was
not in debt at all. When He hung on the cross,
was buried, and rose victorious three days
later, the sinless Jesus fully paid the sin debt
of every human being. Something we could
never repay on our own merit, Jesus repaid
completely. What an act of infinite compassion and incomparable love! Throughout
the Gospels, Jesus demonstrated through
miracles and taught in parables God's divine
compassion and love. What will you do this
Christmas season to show someone God's
compassion and love and thereby the hope of
Christmas?

Who is a God like You,
Pardoning iniquity
And passing over the transgression of the
remnant of His heritage?

He does not retain His anger forever,
Because He delights in mercy.
He will again have compassion on us,
And will subdue our iniquities.

You will cast all our sins
Into the depths of the sea.

Micah 7:18–19

When [Jesus] saw the multitudes, He
was moved with compassion for
them, because they were weary and
scattered, like sheep having no shepherd.

Matthew 9:36

When Jesus went out He saw a
great multitude; and He was
moved with compassion for
them, and healed their sick.

Matthew 14:14

God's Power

———— ✳ ————

What a responsibility! How can flesh and bone—mere "earthen vessels"—possibly shine forth the glory of the living God? We can't—in our own power. But each day, as we faithfully serve Jesus, His Spirit works to mold us more and more into His image. As this process unfolds, people around us can see His light shining in us and through us, and we are able to be God's ambassadors in the world, used by Him to introduce people to the love and grace available to them in Christ. Acting in the power of the Holy Spirit, we can shine forth—in this season and always—the light of hope and joy for the good of those around us and for God's glory!

"Believe Me that I am in the Father and the Father in Me, or else believe Me for the sake of the works themselves. Most assuredly, I say to you, he who believes in Me, the works that I do he will do also; and greater works than these he will do, because I go to My Father. And whatever you ask in My name, that I will do, that the Father may be glorified in the Son."

John 14:11–13

For it is the God who commanded light to shine out of darkness, who has shone in our hearts to give the light of the knowledge of the glory of God in the face of Jesus Christ. But we have this treasure in earthen vessels, that the excellence of the power may be of God and not of us.

2 Corinthians 4:6–7

His Strength

———— ✳ ————

*G*od promises His people strength—the kind of strength Jesus showed as He let Himself be nailed to the cross in submission to God's plan. Even though we know God's immeasurable strength is available to us, our fear—of Satan, of spiritual warfare, or simply of the unknown—may still be very real.

Consider these truths with which you can counter those fears: God is all-powerful. His strength is available 24/7. Whatever our situation, God goes before us, and He is always with us. Nothing is impossible for God. We can accomplish all He asks of us as long as we rely on His strength instead of our own. Even though circumstances of life might appear overwhelming, they are no match for our Savior.

The apparently helpless Babe born in Bethlehem was actually our omnipotent, almighty God in human flesh. In a Christmas card, point someone who needs hope and strength to Him, to the Shield and Refuge, to the Savior.

The LORD is my strength and my shield;
My heart trusted in Him, and I am helped;
Therefore my heart greatly rejoices,
And with my song I will praise Him.

The LORD is their strength,
And He is the saving refuge of His anointed.
Save Your people,
And bless Your inheritance;
Shepherd them also,
And bear them up forever.

Psalm 28:7–9

I can do all things through Christ
who strengthens me.

Philippians 4:13

The LORD is my light and my
*   salvation;*
Whom shall I fear?
The LORD is the strength of my
*   life;*
Of whom shall I be afraid?

Psalm 27:1

God's Presence

～～✳～～

$\mathcal{G}$od's desire for each of us is to live life in His presence. Listening to God is a lifestyle that brings the peace we all yearn for in life. God delights in us when we choose to place our trust in Him. We are the apple of His eye, the object of His special devotion.

If we listen, His Spirit will show the way for us each day. When we let Him guide us continually, we can relax and enjoy the beauty of His presence. When we are close to the One who loves us with an everlasting love, we will find the security, protection, and shelter that only He can give. This is a gift that is available to everyone who chooses to walk with God.

I have set the LORD always before me;
Because He is at my right hand I shall not be
    moved.

Therefore my heart is glad, and my glory
    rejoices;
My flesh also will rest in hope. . . .
You will show me the path of life;
In Your presence is fullness of joy;
At Your right hand are pleasures forevermore.

Psalm 16:8–9, 11

For Christ has not entered the holy
places made with hands, which are
copies of the true, but into heaven
itself, now to appear in the presence
of God for us.

Hebrews 9:24

Surely the righteous shall give
    thanks to Your name;
The upright shall dwell in Your
    presence.

Psalm 140:13

Day 20

His Peace

— ✳ —

The peace of Jesus "surpasses all understanding" (Philippians 4:7) because it has a supernatural source in the heart of Christ Himself. The promise of His peace keeps us from fear and worry because it brings us straight to Him. Christ is our peace, and there is nothing that can separate us from His love, mercy, and grace. How great it is for those who place their faith in the risen Christ! We move from darkness to light, from enemies to beloved children, from death to life. God shows His peace to those who trust Him. The peace that Christ has promised all believers banishes fear and dread from our hearts, for Jesus is in control of all circumstances. Trust in the Lord with all your heart today! He has promised to direct your path.

48

Therefore, having been justified by faith, we have peace with God through our Lord Jesus Christ, through whom also we have access by faith into this grace in which we stand, and rejoice in hope of the glory of God.

Romans 5:1–2

For He Himself is our peace, who has made both one, and has broken down the middle wall of separation, having abolished in His flesh the enmity, that is, the law of commandments contained in ordinances, so as to create in Himself one new man from the two, thus making peace.

Ephesians 2:14–15

The Return of Our Lord

~~~ ✳ ~~~

The return of our Lord and Savior Jesus Christ has been predicted by many people, particularly in this last century. Despite the many attempts to pinpoint the time of Jesus' return, God's Word stands clear: He will come "at an hour you do not expect." Our calling is to remain in a perpetual state of readiness. Jesus promised His disciples that He would not leave them fatherless. He would come to them. He has also promised that He will come again and receive us unto Himself, that where He is we will be also. At the second coming of Jesus, you will see this promise fulfilled. Therefore live each day with anticipation and hope in your heart. When He chooses to return, we who are saved will be with Him in paradise.

"He will give you another Helper . . . the Spirit of truth, whom the world cannot receive, because it neither sees Him nor knows Him; but you know Him, for He dwells with you and will be in you. I will not leave you orphans; I will come to you."

John 14:16–18

"Heaven and earth will pass away, but My words will by no means pass away. But of that day and hour no one knows, not even the angels of heaven, but My Father only. . . . Therefore you also be ready, for the Son of Man is coming at an hour you do not expect."

Matthew 24:35–36, 44

God's Patience

～※～

*P*atience is a lifestyle not easily found in our culture today. We live in a "Hurry up—I want it now" world dominated by technology. Learning to be patient is a difficult lesson. Everyone wants to enjoy the blessings of God's promises *right now*, but unfortunately not everyone will. Lazy believers who exercise neither their faith nor their patience shouldn't expect the abundant satisfaction and peace available because of God's promises. All the more reason to avoid laziness and instant gratification! Each Christian is a work in progress. Let patience be your guide so that you will learn more and live more for the One who gave His life so that you may have life everlasting.

For whatever things were written before were written for our learning, that we through the patience and comfort of the Scriptures might have hope. Now may the God of patience and comfort grant you to be like-minded toward one another, according to Christ Jesus, that you may with one mind and one mouth glorify the God and Father of our Lord Jesus Christ.

Romans 15:4–6

Therefore be patient, brethren, until the coming of the Lord. See how the farmer waits for the precious fruit of the earth, waiting patiently for it until it receives the early and latter rain. You also be patient. Establish your hearts, for the coming of the Lord is at hand.

James 5:7–8

The Abundant Life

~~~ ✳ ~~~

*W*e have a living hope. The resurrection of Jesus guarantees that God will honor all His promises to His faithful children. That hope keeps us going even in the darkest times.

Jesus is not one of many doors leading to the Father; He is the only door. He never claimed to be one route among several to an intimate relationship with God but instead declared that He is the only way. If Jesus willingly gave His life to save ours, how can we think He would ever keep from us anything that would truly benefit us? He is the Good Shepherd, not the stingy shepherd or the tightfisted shepherd. The reality is that God has promised that the abundant Christian life is the Lord Jesus alive within the believer. He *is* our abundant life!

"I am the door. If anyone enters by Me, he will be saved, and will go in and out and find pasture. The thief does not come except to steal, and to kill, and to destroy. I have come that they may have life, and that they may have it more abundantly. I am the good shepherd. The good shepherd gives His life for the sheep."

John 10:9–11

Now to Him who is able to do exceedingly abundantly above all that we ask or think, according to the power that works in us, to Him be glory.

Ephesians 3:20–21

His Love

———※———

*T*he love of God is the most profound gift and promise of the Bible. As He loves us and we love one another, we exemplify our spiritual birth and our relationship with God. God is love, and anyone in whom God dwells will reflect His character. The love of God for His children was visibly demonstrated through Jesus' death on the cross. God's goal for you and me is to be transformed into the image of Christ, to reflect His loving character in our behavior and attitudes so that others may see the love of God in us. Once God has set His love in us and we accept it through faith in Jesus, nothing can ever break the bonds of love He has created. If God, the uncreated One, is for us and no created thing can separate us, then our security in Him is absolute.

Beloved, let us love one another, for love is of God; and everyone who loves is born of God and knows God. He who does not love does not know God, for God is love. In this the love of God was manifested toward us, that God has sent His only begotten Son into the world, that we might live through Him. In this is love, not that we loved God, but that He loved us and sent His Son to be the propitiation for our sins. Beloved, if God so loved us, we also ought to love one another.

1 John 4:7–11

For I am persuaded that neither death nor life, nor angels nor principalities nor powers, nor things present nor things to come, nor height nor depth, nor any other created thing, shall be able to separate us from the love of God which is in Christ Jesus our Lord.

Romans 8:38–39

Our Savior

———— ✳ ————

*T*he angel that announced the Savior told the shepherds not to fear but to open their eyes and look for the good things God was doing for them and for the whole world—things that would bring great joy to everyone.

The object of Christianity is not to sin less but to glorify God more. It is not to stop ourselves from doing the bad things we really want to do but to find ourselves craving to do what pleases God.

As we celebrate the hope of our Savior during this Christmas season, we are encouraged to glorify God by caring for the ones we love, to reach out and find ourselves longing to please God by serving others. During this season, show the love of Christ. It may be the best gift anyone could receive.

Then the angel said to them, "Do not be afraid, for behold, I bring you good tidings of great joy which will be to all people. For there is born to you this day in the city of David a Savior, who is Christ the Lord?"

Luke 2:10–11

We should live . . . looking for the blessed hope and glorious appearing of our great God and Savior Jesus Christ.

Titus 2:12–13

God's Wisdom

———— ✳ ————

When God invited Solomon to ask for whatever he wanted, the king requested wisdom (1 Kings 3:9). That God-given wisdom taught Solomon that only a fool tries to solve problems without God's help. Any time we spend wondering how to get out of a touchy situation is time wasted. God's guidance is more than sufficient for all the tests or trials we might face, regardless of the package in which the test comes wrapped. God has promised in His Word that He will provide all the wisdom we will ever need, if only we will come to Him and ask for it.

*"Abide in Me, and I in you. As the branch
cannot bear fruit of itself, unless it abides in
the vine, neither can you, unless you abide in
Me. I am the vine, you are the branches. He
who abides in Me, and I in him, bears much
fruit; for without Me you can do nothing. If
anyone does not abide in Me, he is cast out
as a branch and is withered; and they gather
them and throw them into the fire, and they
are burned. If you abide in Me, and My words
abide in you, you will ask what you desire,
and it shall be done for you."*

John 15:4–7

*Trust in the LORD with all your
heart,
And lean not on your own
understanding;
In all your ways acknowledge
Him,
And He shall direct your paths.*

Proverbs 3:5–6

The Holy Spirit

———— ✳ ————

*W*ith a sound like a violent wind and amid flames of fire, the long-promised Holy Spirit arrived on the day of Pentecost. The disciples and other Christ-followers witnessed His undeniable presence and continue to do so even today as He gives comfort, wisdom, and power to those who name Jesus as their Lord and Savior.

Once we name Jesus as Lord and receive His Spirit, we then choose daily—if not moment by moment—whether to live in the Spirit, whether to depend on His power, follow His direction, and rely on Him to help us die to self. When we make that choice to walk with the Spirit—when we choose to let Him guide us along the narrow path of loving, joyful, and freeing friendship with Christ—others will glimpse in us what God is like. And by the Spirit's power, we can resist the temptations of the world, stand strong in God's truth, keep our eyes on the Lord Jesus, and know in our heart of hearts *the true promise of Christmas.*

"The Helper, the Holy Spirit, whom the Father will send in My name, He will teach you all things, and bring to your remembrance all things that I said to you."

John 14:26

"You shall receive power when the Holy Spirit has come upon you; and you shall be witnesses to Me in Jerusalem, and in all Judea and Samaria, and to the end of the earth." . . . *And when they had prayed, the place where they were assembled together was shaken; and they were all filled with the Holy Spirit, and they spoke the word of God with boldness.*

Acts 1:8; 4:31

Abundance from Above

~~~ ✴ ~~~

*O*pportunities to give are all around us, at this time of the year more than at any other. Do you feel a pang of guilt that you can't do more? Or on a smaller scale, if you receive a gift and don't have one to give in return? We selfish, self-centered human beings expect our giving to be reciprocated. Why give if we have nothing to gain?

God, however, has a very different perspective on giving because divine love is different. Christlike love gives unselfishly and expects nothing in return. Yet because we love God, we want to respond to His gifts. There is no way we could ever repay all He has given to us, but we can give to others our talents, energy, time, and money to demonstrate God's love in our lives—to pay it forward. To whom and how will you pay forward God's unselfish love this season?

Let each one give as he purposes in his heart, not grudgingly or of necessity; for God loves a cheerful giver. And God is able to make all grace abound toward you, that you, always having all sufficiency in all things, may have an abundance for every good work.

2 Corinthians 9:7–8

For you know the grace of our Lord Jesus Christ, that though He was rich, yet for your sakes He became poor, that you through His poverty might become rich.

2 Corinthians 8:9

Eternal Life

~~~ ✳ ~~~

*E*arly-bird specials. Doorbusters. Lowest-price-of-the-season sales. The ads are everywhere—but what if you came across one that said "Free Ticket to Heaven"? You check the fine print: "Limited time offer. Must redeem before you die. Sinners only."

Of course, you don't need a ticket to enter heaven. But Jesus, by His sacrificial death on the cross for our sins, does offer the gift of eternal life to all of us sinners, and we do need to receive it before we die. Now, eternal life does not mean we simply go to heaven and live forever, although that alone would be spectacular. It means we enjoy an eternal friendship with Jesus—starting the very moment we accept Him as Savior! We will continue in heaven the relationship with Jesus we begin here on earth.

Sharing your excitement about your friendship with the Savior will lead others to wonder what is different about your life and to want it for themselves. And they will find in

Jesus the gift of eternal life (it begins now) and the promise of Christmas (it lasts forever).

Having been set free from sin, and having become slaves of God, you have your fruit to holiness, and the end, everlasting life. For the wages of sin is death, but the gift of God is eternal life in Christ Jesus our Lord.

Romans 6:22–23

Let that abide in you which you heard from the beginning. If what you heard from the beginning abides in you, you also will abide in the Son and in the Father. And this is the promise that He has promised us—eternal life. . . . And this is the testimony: that God has given us eternal life, and this life is in His Son. He who has the Son has life; he who does not have the Son of God does not have life.

1 John 2:24–25; 5:11–12

The Gift of Prayer

~~~ ✳ ~~~

hroughout the Bible, God promises to speak to His children. But we must listen for His voice. Key to such active listening is going before the Lord expectantly. Eagerly anticipating His words to us will prime our hearts and minds to hear Him. And this kind of prayer dialogue is essential to our relationship with God—the almighty One who knows our names and numbers the hairs on our heads. All-loving and utterly compassionate, He desires to have us share with Him our innermost thoughts and feelings, our dreams and fears, our regrets and hopes. Our Creator God—our heavenly Father—wants to hear from us when the road is rough as well as when it is smooth. Sweet times of prayer happen when we go before Him with praise, worshipping and giving thanks for what He has done. Prayer is the breath of our spiritual life. We can go to God as often as we like each day, and we will be blessed.

Be anxious for nothing, but in everything by prayer and supplication, with thanksgiving, let your requests be made known to God; and the peace of God, which surpasses all understanding, will guard your hearts and minds through Christ Jesus.

Philippians 4:6–7

Now may the Lord of peace Himself give you peace always in every way. The Lord be with you all. . . . The grace of our Lord Jesus Christ be with you all. Amen.

2 Thessalonians 3:16, 18

Confess your trespasses to one another, and pray for one another, that you may be healed. The effective, fervent prayer of a righteous man avails much.

James 5:16

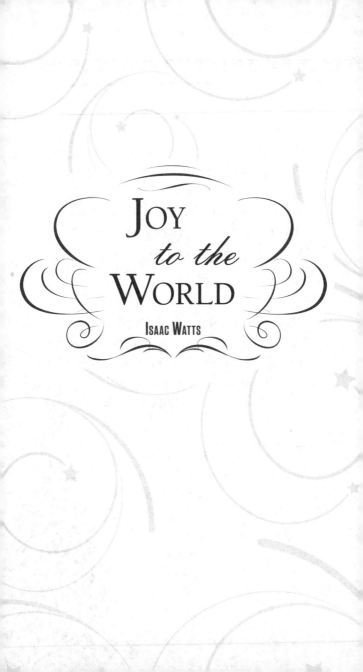

Joy to the world, the Lord is come! Let earth receive her King.
Let every heart prepare Him room,
And heaven and nature sing, and heaven and nature sing,
And heaven, and heaven and nature sing.

Joy to the earth, the Savior reigns! Let men their songs employ,
While fields and floods, rocks, hills and plains
Repeat the sounding joy, repeat the sounding joy,
Repeat, repeat the sounding joy.

No more let sin and sorrow grow, nor thorns infest the ground.
He comes to make His blessings flow
Far as the curse is found, far as the curse is found,
Far as, far as the curse is found.

He rules the world with truth and grace and makes the nations prove
The glories of His righteousness
And wonders of His love, and wonders of His love,
And wonders, and wonders of His love.